The Velveteen Rabbit
COLORING BOOK

Based on the Story by Margery Williams

Adapted by Sally Green

Illustrations by Michael Green

Adapted by Neesa Becker

RUNNING PRESS
Philadelphia, Pennsylvania

 Canadian representatives: General Publishing Co., Ltd., 30 Lesmill Road, Don Mills, Ontario M3B 2T6. ISBN 0-89471-449-X. Cover design by Toby Schmidt. Cover illustration by Michael Green. Typography: American Classic by rci, Philadelphia, Pennsylvania. Printed by Port City Press, Baltimore, Maryland. This book may be ordered directly by mail from the publisher. Please add $2.50 for postage and handling for each copy. *But try your bookstore first!* Running Press Book Publishers, 125 South Twenty-second Street, Philadelphia, Pennsylvania 19103.
9 8 7 6 5 4
The digit on the right indicates the number of this printing.

There was once a velveteen rabbit. On Christmas morning he sat wedged in the Boy's stocking. His coat was spotted brown and white, he had real thread whiskers, and his ears were lined with pink sateen.

There were other presents, but the Boy loved him quite the best of all. Then in all the Christmas excitement, the little Rabbit was forgotten.

For a long time he lived neglected in the nursery. The more expensive mechanical toys, who acted very superior, pretended they were real and looked down on him. Being naturally shy and only made of velveteen, the poor little Rabbit felt very insignificant and commonplace. The only person who was kind to him was the Skin Horse.

The Skin Horse was very old and wise and understood all about nursery magic. "What is REAL?" the Rabbit asked him one day.

''Real isn't how you're made. It's a thing that happens to you. When a child loves you for a long, long time, not just to play with, but REALLY loves you, then you become Real,'' he answered. ''And sometimes it hurts,'' the Skin Horse said, for he was always truthful. ''But when you are Real you don't mind.

''Becoming Real takes a long time. By then, most of your hair has been loved off and you get very shabby. But these things don't matter at all.''

''I suppose you're Real,'' said the Rabbit.

The Skin Horse smiled and said, ''The Boy's Uncle made me Real; and once you're Real, it lasts for always.''

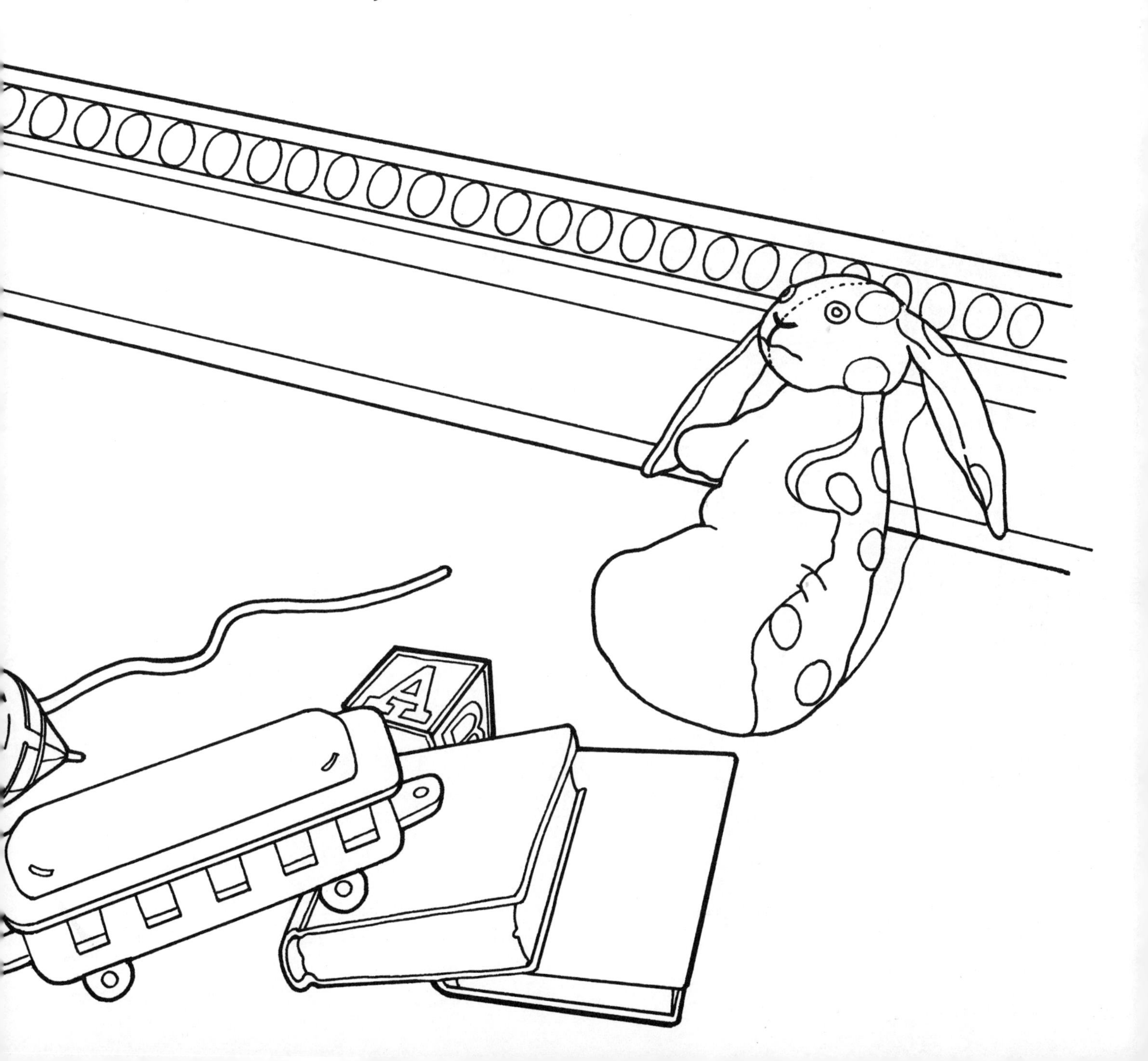

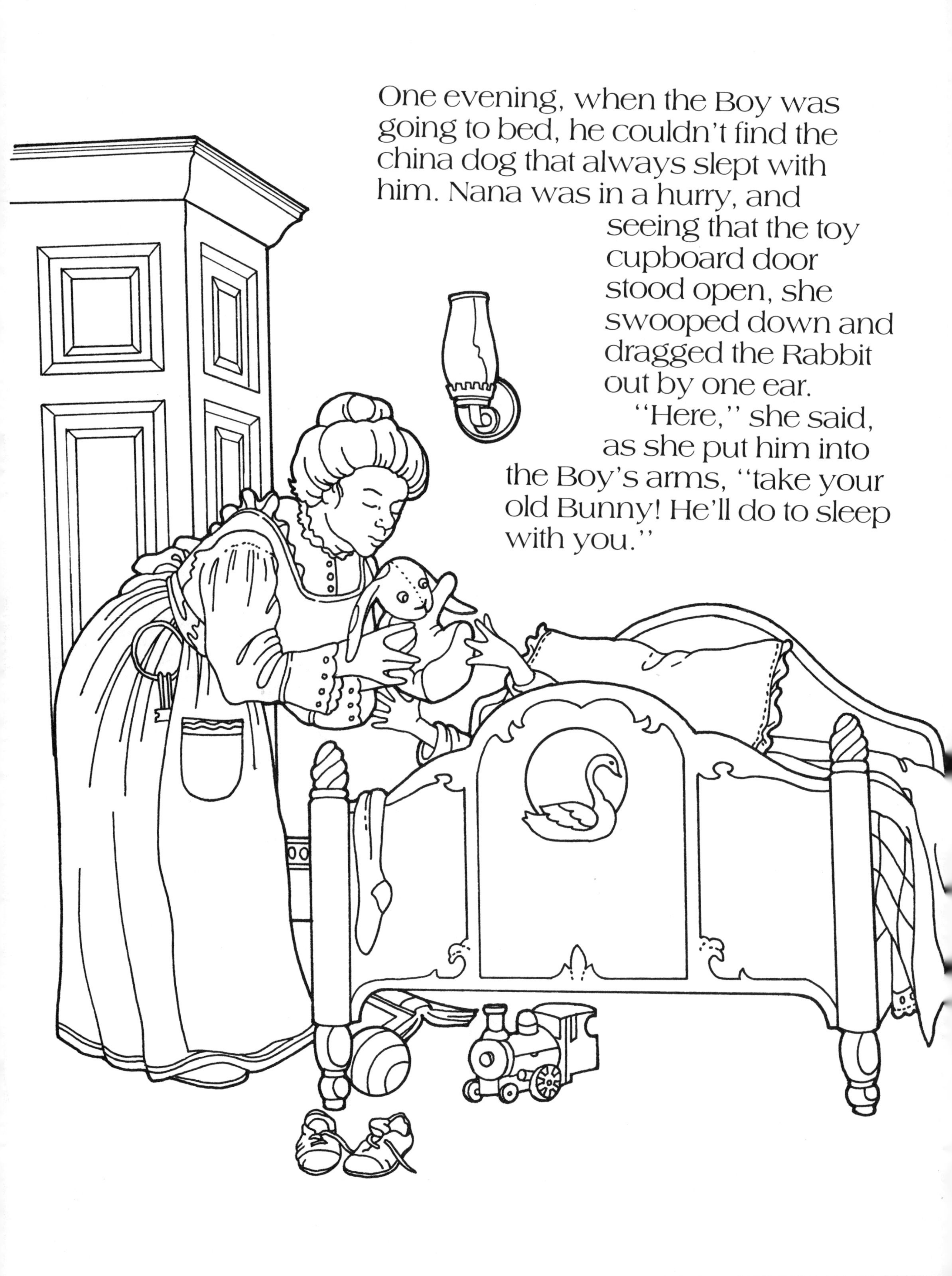

One evening, when the Boy was going to bed, he couldn't find the china dog that always slept with him. Nana was in a hurry, and seeing that the toy cupboard door stood open, she swooped down and dragged the Rabbit out by one ear.

"Here," she said, as she put him into the Boy's arms, "take your old Bunny! He'll do to sleep with you."

A
O
D

For many nights after, the Velveteen Rabbit slept in the Boy's bed. They had splendid games together, in whispers, when Nana had gone away and left the nightlight burning.

And when the Boy dropped off to sleep, the Rabbit would happily snuggle under his little warm chin and dream, with the Boy's hands clasped close round him all night long.

Spring came, and they had long days in the garden, for wherever the Boy went the Rabbit went too. He had rides —in the wheelbarrow—

— and picnics on the grass, and the Boy built lovely fairy huts for him under the raspberry canes behind the flower border.

Once, when the Boy was called away suddenly,
the Rabbit was left out on the lawn until long after dusk.
He was wet through with dew and quite earthy from
diving into the burrows the Boy had made for him in the
flower bed.

Nana had to come look for him with a candle because the Boy couldn't go to sleep unless he was there. She grumbled as she rubbed him off with a corner of her apron.

"You must have your old Bunny!" she said. "Fancy all that fuss for a toy!"

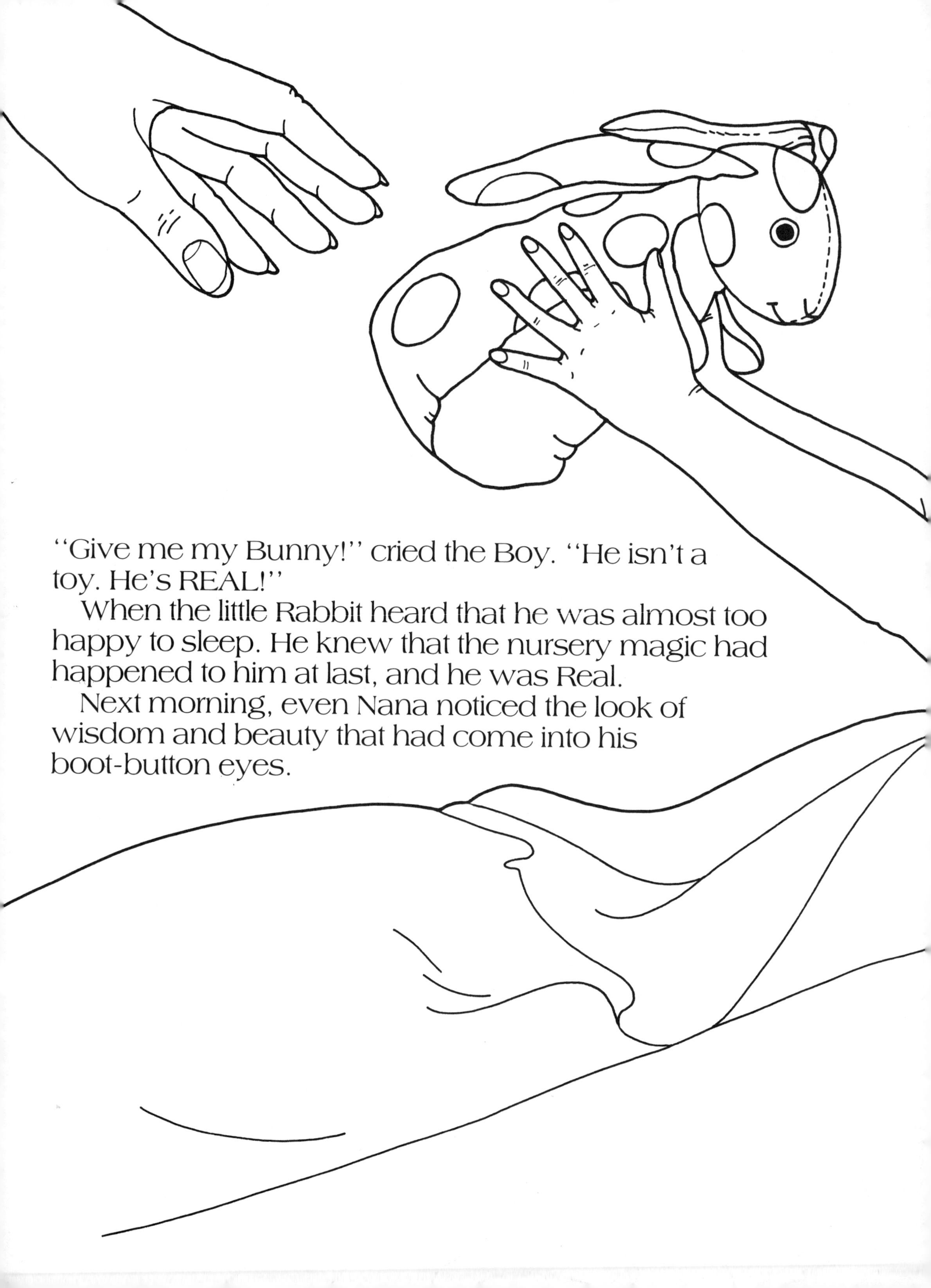

"Give me my Bunny!" cried the Boy. "He isn't a toy. He's REAL!"

When the little Rabbit heard that he was almost too happy to sleep. He knew that the nursery magic had happened to him at last, and he was Real.

Next morning, even Nana noticed the look of wisdom and beauty that had come into his boot-button eyes.

That was a wonderful summer!

In the long June evenings the Boy liked to take the Velveteen Rabbit to play in the wood. Because he was kindhearted, he always made the Rabbit a cosy little nest while he wandered off to pick flowers, or play.

Once, when the Rabbit was alone, he saw some strange beings creep out of the tall ferns.

They were rabbits like himself, but quite furry and brand-new. They changed shape in a queer way when they moved, instead of always staying the same like he did. He stared hard to see the wind-up clockwork that made them jump, but he couldn't see it. They were evidently a new kind of rabbit altogether.

"Come play!" one of them called.

"I don't feel like it," said the Rabbit, for he didn't want to explain he had no clockwork inside. But wild rabbits have very sharp eyes, and one declared, "He's got no hind legs! He's not real!"

"I *am* Real!" he cried. He felt he would give anything to be able to jump about. And he nearly began to cry.

Weeks passed, and the little Rabbit grew very old and shabby from being loved so hard by the Boy. He scarcely looked like a rabbit any more. But to the Boy he was always beautiful, and that's all the little Rabbit cared about. The nursery magic had made him Real, and when you're Real shabbiness doesn't matter.

And then, one day, the Boy was ill. His body was burning with scarlet fever. The little Rabbit knew the Boy couldn't play, so he just snuggled down under the blankets.

Finally the Boy got better. In the morning he was going to the seaside. The Doctor ordered his room disinfected and all the toys in his bed burned.

The little Rabbit was put into a sack with the other toys and carried outside to be burned. He felt very sad as he wriggled his head out to look at the place where he had played with the Boy. He thought, "What use is it to be loved —and become Real—if it all ends like this?"

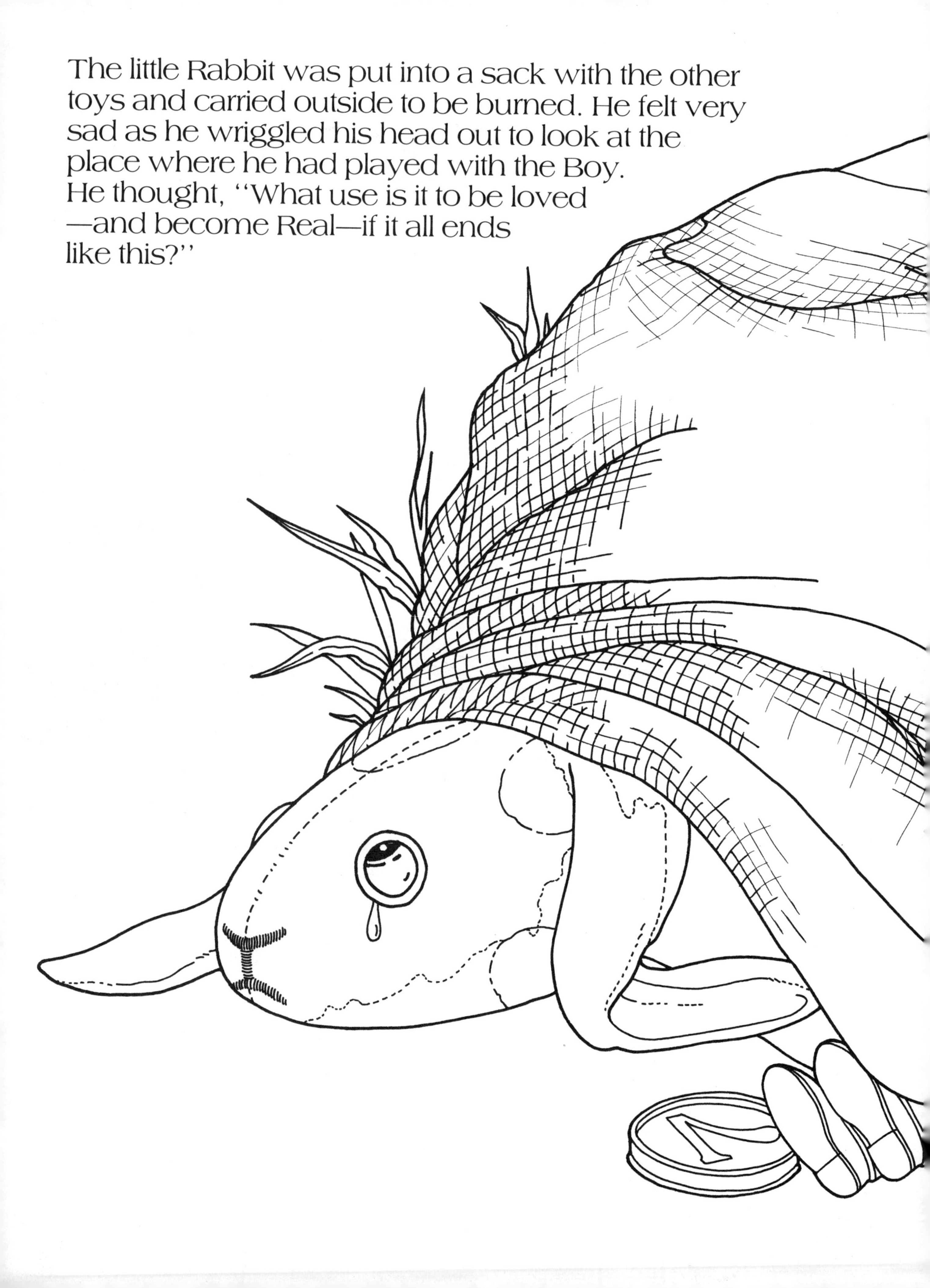

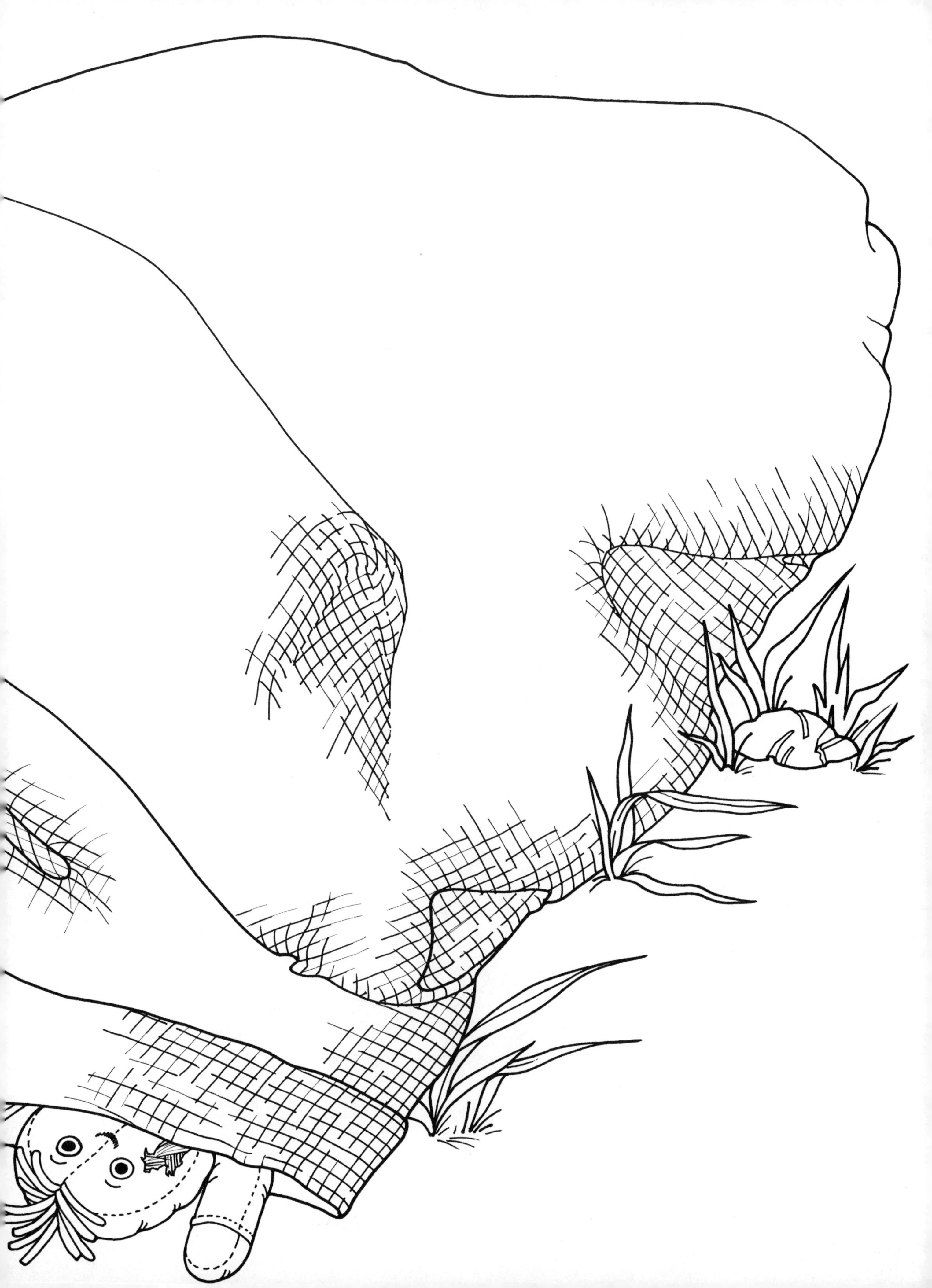

Then a tear, a real tear, trickled down his nose. And a strange thing happened. Where the tear fell, a mysterious flower grew up out of the ground. Its leaves were the color of emeralds and its blossom like a golden cup. It was so beautiful that the Rabbit forgot to cry. Then the blossom opened, and out stepped a fairy.

She was the loveliest fairy in the
whole world and she gathered the little Rabbit
up in her arms and kissed him on his damp nose.

"Don't you know who I am?" she said. "I'm the nursery magic Fairy. I take care of all the playthings children have loved. You were Real to the Boy. Now you shall be real to everyone."

Holding the Rabbit close, she flew to an open glade in the wood. The moon had risen and the wild rabbits were dancing. They all stopped when they saw the Fairy.

"I've brought you a new playfellow," she said. "Be kind to him and teach him well."

Then she kissed him, put him down on the grass and said, "Run and play, little Rabbit."

But the little Rabbit sat quite still, not wanting the others to see he was made all in one piece. Suddenly, his nose tickled and he lifted a hind toe to scratch it.

When he found he actually had hind legs, soft fur, and twitching ears, he took a great leap for joy. At last, he was a real Rabbit.

Winter passed, and in the Spring, when the days grew warm, the Boy went out to play in the wood. While he was playing, two rabbits crept out from the ferns and peeped at him. One of them was brown all over, but the other had strange markings under his fur, as though long ago he had been spotted, and the spots still showed through.

About his little soft nose and his round black eyes there was something familiar, so that the Boy thought to himself:

"Why, he looks just like my old Bunny that was lost when I had scarlet fever!"

But he never knew that it really was his own Bunny, come back to look at the child who had first helped him to be Real.